One day with
the Aborigines

DAY BOOK SERIES

Acknowledgements

We should like to express our gratitude to all those who have kindly granted copyright permission for photographs in this volume, and special thanks to our illustrators.

Australian News and Information Bureau: pages 8 (top), 10, 12, 13 (top), 14 (bottom), 15 (bottom), 16, 17, 18, 19, 22 (top), 23, 24 (left), 25 (right), 28, 30, 31, 32, 33 (top), 35 (top), 36, 37 (bottom), 39 (right), 42

Graham Cowles: pages 7 (top), 20, 26, 27, 34 (top)

Educational Productions Ltd., Wakefield, Yorks.:
From the filmstrip: Everyday Life Among the Australian Aborigines, pages 11 (bottom), 15 (top), 24–25 (centre), 39 (top left)

The Mansell Collection: pages 38 (bottom), 40, 41 (top)

The Royal Geographical Society: pages 7 (bottom), 34 (bottom), 35 (bottom), 41 (bottom)

Richard Hook: illustrations, pages 5, 21, 29

Cecilia Ware: line drawings, pages 4, 8 (bottom), 9, 11, 14 (top), 22 (bottom), 33 (bottom), 37 (top), 38 (top)

First Edition 1974
Second Edition 1976

© 1976 ROBERT TYNDALL

Published in South Africa by Robert Tyndall (Pty) Ltd

ISBN 85949 039 4

Printed and bound in Spain by
Novograph S.A. and Roner S.A., Madrid
D.L.: M 37361/1975

One day with the Aborigines

by Michael Hobbs

TYNDALL

Opposite, left to right:
Marbogwa, Natanya, Wirri,
Barrimba,
Bimba,
Chimbani, Anfrani, Kinshari

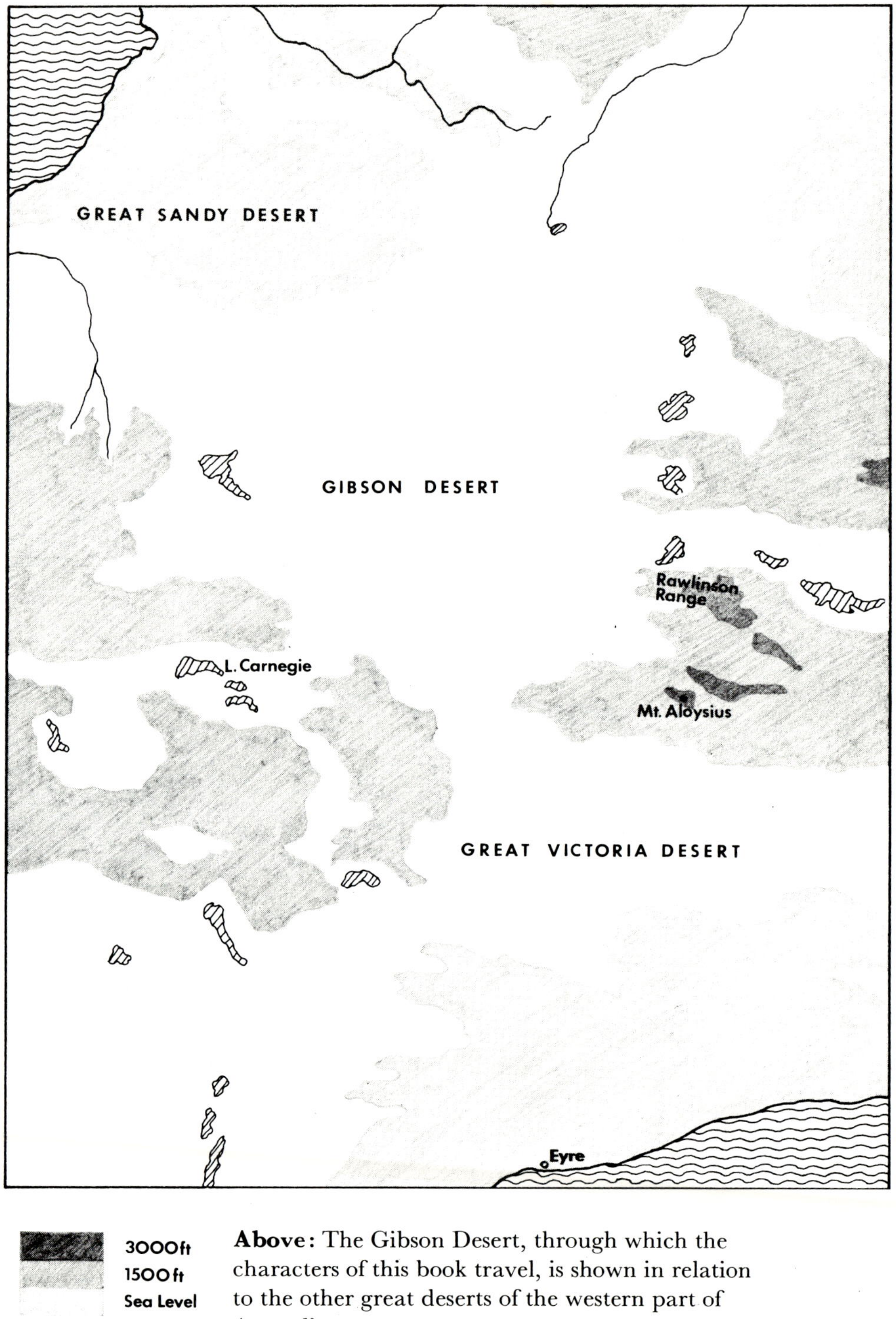
GREAT SANDY DESERT
GIBSON DESERT
Rawlinson Range
L. Carnegie
Mt. Aloysius
GREAT VICTORIA DESERT
Eyre
3000ft
1500ft
Sea Level

Above: The Gibson Desert, through which the characters of this book travel, is shown in relation to the other great deserts of the western part of Australia

Contents

Introduction   6
MORNING   7
AFTERNOON   26
EVENING   35
Glossary   43
General Notes   45
Index   46
Further Reading   48

AD 1920

Introduction

Life with the Australian desert Aborigines is a subject about which, sadly, we hear relatively little. Sadly, because their simple, day-to-day existence together with their age-old customs form a singular balance between the routine and the ritual of life.

History is fun; but a list of unconnected accounts of battles and events is not.

History is the story of how we, the human race, governed, fought, learned and lived in years gone by. The influence of one people upon another, and often of one man upon a nation, is crucial to the development of civilisation.

In this series, we look at the customs and events of an age, and history is shown through the eyes of those who were living at the time.

The series is intended as an introduction to a period, and great care has been taken to see that all illustrations, photographs and artwork are accurate. Where an illustration is not specifically from the year in which the book is set, the caption explains its relevance and, wherever possible, its date.

Words in italics in the text (italicised only at their first appearance) are explained in the Glossary, and there is further information on some aspects of the times in the General Notes. An Index is provided for easy reference, but it is recommended that the book be read as a whole to begin with.

Having had a taste of the atmosphere of the age, you may be interested to read more about some of the people, their homes, politics, literature, society, religious beliefs and customs. There is a Further Reading list at the back of the book, but this represents only a small number of the many books available. Have a look in your library and see what you can find.

MORNING

Desert stars in thousands, shining in the clear chill air, dimly outlined a group of figures around the still embers of a fire. In the east, the sky slowly paled until, quite suddenly, the dull orange of the sun began to slide into view, away across the flat and arid landscape.

Marbogwa moved in sleep, grunting as the early light touched his eyelids. Unhurried and smoothly, he rose to his feet, and now fully awake he scanned the landscape. As yet nothing moved and his eyes saw only stony flatness, given life by an occasional cluster of low rounded rocks. Also, about a mile away, were some dusty grey-green bushes that followed the course of a dry *creek* bed, which had not carried water for several years. Satisfied that there was no threat in the new day, he looked back to his sleeping family. Wirri, his fourteen-year-old daughter and the eldest of his four children, was uncomfortable, and wriggled her shoulders on the hard ground, her lips half smiling as she dreamed.

With the sun three-quarters above the horizon, it was time for the day to begin for them all. Marbogwa went over to his wife Natanya and pushed her gently in the stomach with his foot. Mumbling, she turned away from him, so he squatted on his haunches and shook her more

Above: Typical Gibson Desert scenery, showing also a rock shelter which many desert Aborigines make use of
Below: Aborigines encamped at a waterhole

7

Above: The goanna (*Varanus varius*) is a black
and yellow lizard which grows to a length of
six feet, and sometimes more

Below: The Aborigine method of making fire
by drilling with a firestick into a dry piece of wood

firmly now by the shoulders. At once she awoke and pushed herself up from the bare ground.

'Come,' he said, 'we must quickly eat and drink what is left and go to the next waterhole before the heat.' Natanya stood up and moved hastily round the children, waking them. Each would have a task to do before they left this place. Wirri was awake instantly and went over to the remains of the fire. Although the severest of the night chill had left the air, her unclothed body still craved warmth; and it would improve the remains of the *goannas* they had eaten the night before if she could heat them a little. The few pieces of lizard that were left would put strength in them for the long hard day ahead. They would be lucky to eat again that day.

Barrimba joined her at the fire. He placed his *woomera* on the ground. Holding it firmly under one foot, and using a *firestick* between his stretched and tensed fingers, he began to drill firmly down into the dry hard wood of the *spearthrower*.

'Look, we don't need a new fire,' said Wirri. She had been blowing gently and steadily through cupped hands on the near-cold ashes and blackened twigs. Smoke began to rise again and a few small flames flickered. 'Get more wood,' she shouted. Nodding, Barrimba began to gather the twisted grey dead wood, the remains of a *mulga* bush they had decided to save for the morning's fire.

Marbogwa reappeared smiling happily for he had had good luck. Climbing up a rock to plan the route they would follow that day, he had come upon a goanna. Lizards are slow to move until their blood is warmed by the sun, so he was able to snatch it up as it ran – rather than flashed – towards the safety of its crack in the rock.

'We shall eat well now,' he said, holding the prize above his head so that all could see. The goanna was much larger than those they usually caught, more than three feet long. Quickly he snapped its neck and tossed the creature over to Natanya. The hunter's job was done and the rest was up to the women. Natanya squatted on her haunches in the easy way natural to primitive races, and searched quickly among the stones around her. She picked up some, and then discarded them when they did not meet her needs. Finally she chose a *flint* broken quite recently and therefore with an edge sharp enough for her purpose; she began to half cut, half saw, at the soft warm belly of the goanna. If she removed the skin they could make use of it later, and the flesh would cook more quickly. Her two youngest children, Kinshari, who was nearly seven, and Bimba, only three but already a boy who could walk throughout the hottest day without complaint, stood and watched her.

'Bimba! Kinshari!' Marbogwa was calling and pointing. They looked down at the ground, following the direction of his pointing forefinger. There seemed to be nothing.

'What is it?' said Kinshari.

'Look closely, girl.'

She knelt and stared again, more intently this time, and saw what he meant. There were the faint twisting marks in the thin covering of greyish sandy soil that made her say:

'Snake.'

'Of course, but when was it here?'

Kinshari looked at the track carefully, her face only a few inches from the ground. It was important to remember all she had learned of the other tracks she had seen. Memories of the snakes caught or lost since the time her parents had first begun to teach her, when she could barely walk, came back to her. She moved away from them a little, following the track until it crossed a slight hollow. Here the track was clearer in the half-inch-deep soil but, although there had been no wind to smooth the track, its first sharpness had gone.

'We are too late. I think it was here one or maybe two days ago.' Marbogwa nodded in agreement. 'Right, but follow the track. Maybe you will find another snake where that one slept the night before. There could have been enough wind while we slept to smooth out his track.'

Kinshari got to her feet and began to trail, Bimba following. As they moved away, their heads bent in close attention, the last of the family group had woken. Aged and less eager for new days, Chimbani, their grandfather, was sitting up and moving his shoulder, kneading it with long probing fingers, complaining to himself as he did so. The old spear wound had been a deep one, and his shoulder

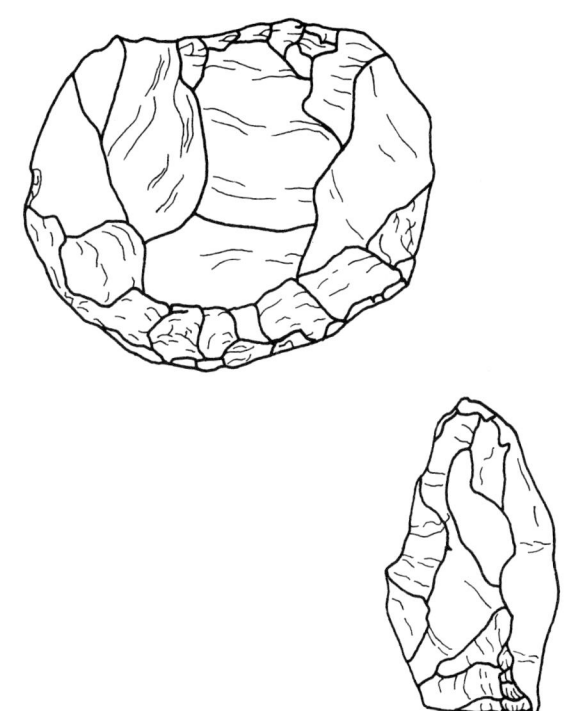

An example of the sort of flint Natanya would have selected for removing the skin of the goanna and preparing the meat for cooking

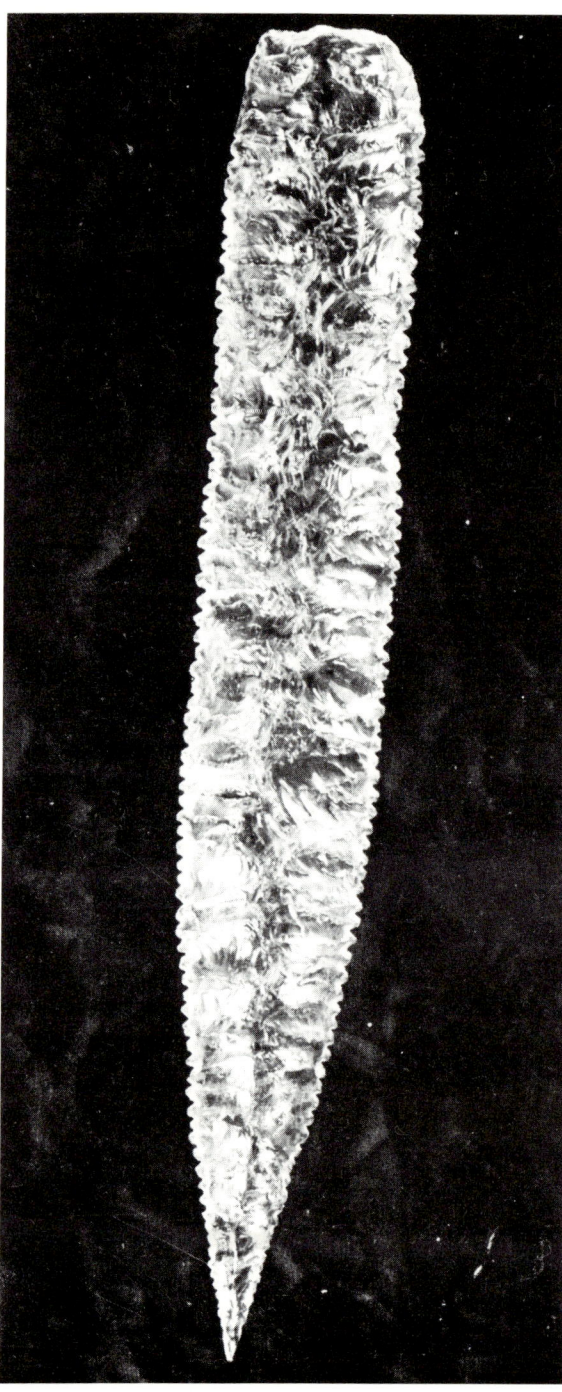

Spearheads were sometimes formed with barbed flints, such as the one shown above. However, often they were merely made of hardwood, tempered with fire

had always given trouble since that tribal fight over a wife his brother had stolen. This had happened before white men had come to punish the stealing of wives and fighting. As the stiffness eased, he considered how silly the whole thing had been.

When the fight was over no one was dead, but many had bruised heads, and Chimbani suffered with a barbed-flint spearhead in his throwing shoulder. The older men had sat and discussed the matter, after which the handing over of three good spear-shafts and a throwing stick had settled everything. The husband did not want his wife anyway. She had borne him no children, had no great skill with her hands or knowledge of the bush, and was possessed of a bitter tongue. When he realized that she was no longer his, he had told the others with a smile that he had three more useful and companionable wives, and one of them a beauty. But the honour of the group demanded that some attempt be made to get her back. After the first clash, however, both sides withdrew to think out the next move. Talk was preferable to blood-shed.

Chimbani looked over at Anfrani. The prettiness that had led his brother, long dead of a snake bite, to want her, was long gone but her tongue had not lost its edge.

'Come, old woman, time to move your bent bones,' he called roughly. This first challenge of the day began their usual round of insults. He generally got the worst of it.

'You wake only to fill your slack belly Chimbani,' Anfrani answered sharply, 'You're no good for anything but that. Your eyes don't see the tracks of our food, and your arm is too weak for the spear. My bones may be bent but without the women to find you seeds and berries and fruit you would die.'

But Chimbani was not drawn into the quarrel. Although all of them could shape a spearhead from flint, *obsidian* and *chert*, or decorate a woomera or a *totem*, he was the acknowledged craftsman of the group. To remind Anfrani of this no words were needed; he only pointed at the spears lying near where Marbogwa had slept that night. He had made them all. However Anfrani's remarks had reminded him that there was a job to do before they left camp. Marbogwa, missing his cast at a kangaroo the day before,

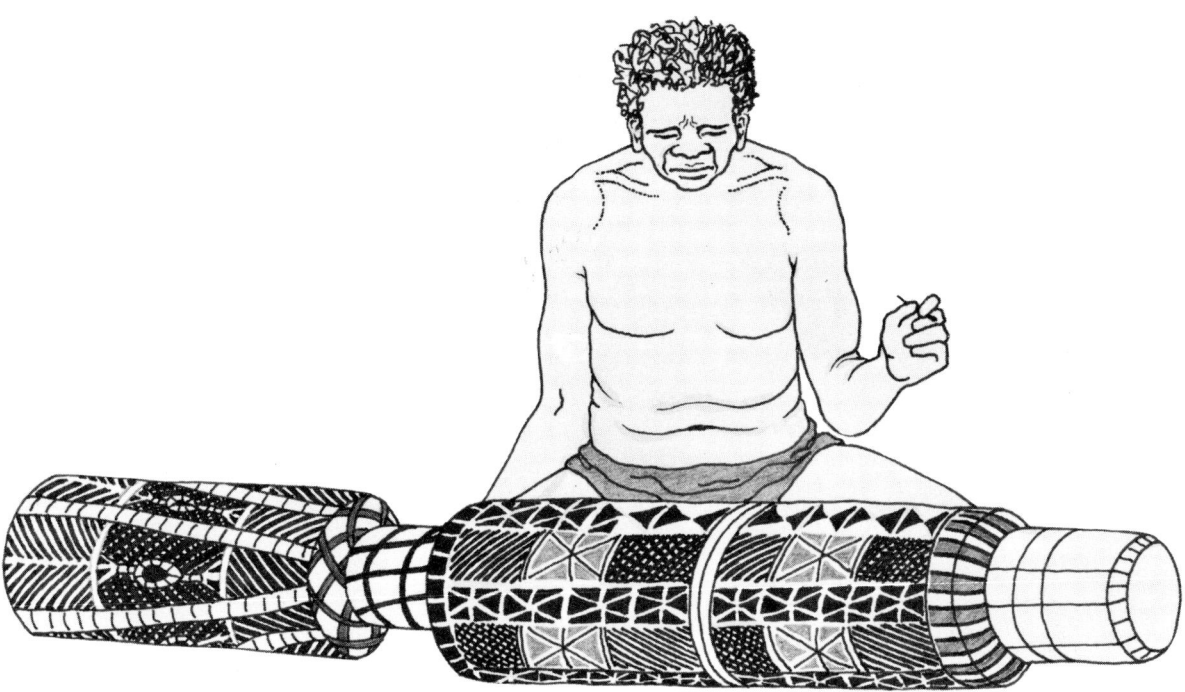

To the Australian Aborigine his totem, or emblem is an extremely important part of his everyday life, and this totem is often symbolized by very intricate paintings or wood carvings. The above illustration shows an Aborigine decorating a totem pole

had broken the shaft of his favourite spear and it must be replaced. Paying no further attention to Anfrani, he picked up a fire-tempered *ironwood* digging stick and strode off towards the creek. He had noticed in the dusk of the previous night a *tjawu* tree there, which should have just the kind of root he needed for a true shaft.

By now, Kinshari and Bimba had tracked the snake as far as the creek, for which Chimbani was making too. At times they had lost the trail when it had slid over sand-blasted, smooth rocks or ground swept bare by desert winds. Each time they had regained the trail by casting round in broad semi-circles, hoping to cross the trail again if the snake had changed direction. Now the track had come to an end at a low, flat slab of rock. The snake must either be lying curled in sleep beneath, or have gone for ever. Softly they approached, quickening with the last few strides. Without speaking, they separated so that each could grasp an end of the rock and lift it away in one movement. For a moment the rock resisted, sinking into the fine, drifted sand of the creek bed, but then it began to move upwards. There was a flash of brown and the snake

Lake Eyre in Central Australia is normally a vast, dry salt-encrusted lake-bed, mostly below sea-level. Discovered by the explorer Edward John Eyre, the area is usually only inhabited by nomadic Aborigines. However, during the winter of 1950 (thirty years later than the date of this story), exceptionally heavy rains in the Queensland watersheds, over 1000 miles away, transformed the area into a gigantic inland sea. This, in its turn, brought an abundance of birds and wildlife in general to the area. The above photograph taken from a height of about 4000 feet, shows the Cooper River entering Lake Eyre during the 1950 flooding

was past them. They turned in pursuit, closing fast on the snake as it desperately sought a place of safety, but losing several yards on it each time it shot away in a new direction. Unexpectedly, the snake gave them their chance. It sighted a cluster of rocks which would no doubt contain a fissure in which it could find safety; but the rocks were about thirty yards away over flat, open ground. Immediately Kinshari began to gain on the creature, her long legs spanning the ground. She drew level with the snake and flung herself sideways in a sprawl over it. She scrabbled persistently and succeeded in pressing her left foot down on its lashing body, while her hand flung out to catch its neck and head. As her hand closed on its smooth dry skin, she bent her head, her teeth sinking a killing bite at the base of the skull. A shudder, and the snake was still. Their breakfast would be a feast.

'Fine hunting for a woman,' called Chimbani, working busily by his chosen ironwood tree. Delighted, the children ran to him, Bimba swinging the snake above his head and then whirling it through the air to land at the old man's feet. 'What are you doing?' Bimba asked. 'Finding a spear,' Chimbani grunted, and returned to his digging. After a while he muttered that it was too short, and again squatted on his heels a little way from the previous spot, thrusting into the fine sand and pausing to scoop it away when his stick had loosened it. Soon a long curling root was exposed, and with a steady pull he was able to drag the end from the ground.

'Good. Now I need an axe,' Chimbani said. He inspected the creek bed for the rough tool that he needed: an edged flint that would fit the hand. But the flints and stones were too well smoothed and rounded, by thousands of years of tumbling and pounding in the *flash floods* which swept down for a few hours, and then seeped away into the desert sands. Instead, he selected two fist-sized nuggets of flint and walked over to a flat rock. Squatting beside it he placed one flint on the rock, and began to strike it with measured glancing blows. At the third attempt a long clean flake split away. He turned the flint over and removed a flake opposite the first. He now had a tool sharp enough for his purpose and quickly hacked through the root, finally snapping it off with his hands.

'Bimba, make a fire,' he said. Squatting again, he brushed the loose soil from the root and began to strip the bark from it with his teeth. Bimba was having difficulty making a fire. He was too young to spin the firestick fast enough, or to bear down with it hard enough on the powder-dry limb of mulga wood, whereas Chimbani soon had the wood-dust smoking, and dry grasses and twigs completed the fire. While the flames died away to leave the glowing embers Chimbani needed, he removed the raised scars from the root with the hand-axe, and then scraped down the thicker end so that his spear-shaft would be the same thickness all along. When the embers were ready, he began the job of straightening and tempering it. As he heated each bend and turn in the root, the wood became pliable and he was easily able to straighten it. Soon he had a straight shaft about twelve feet long. He continued passing it closely over the embers, making the sap sizzle. When the sound ceased, the sap was gone and the wood fully tempered. Now for the point. Chimbani considered whether to make a slim, leaf-shaped point from

Above: Some stone axes made by Aborigines are more sophisticated than the one Chimbani makes in the story. The one illustrated has the stone head fixed between two sticks.
Below: An Aborigine from northern Australia making fire

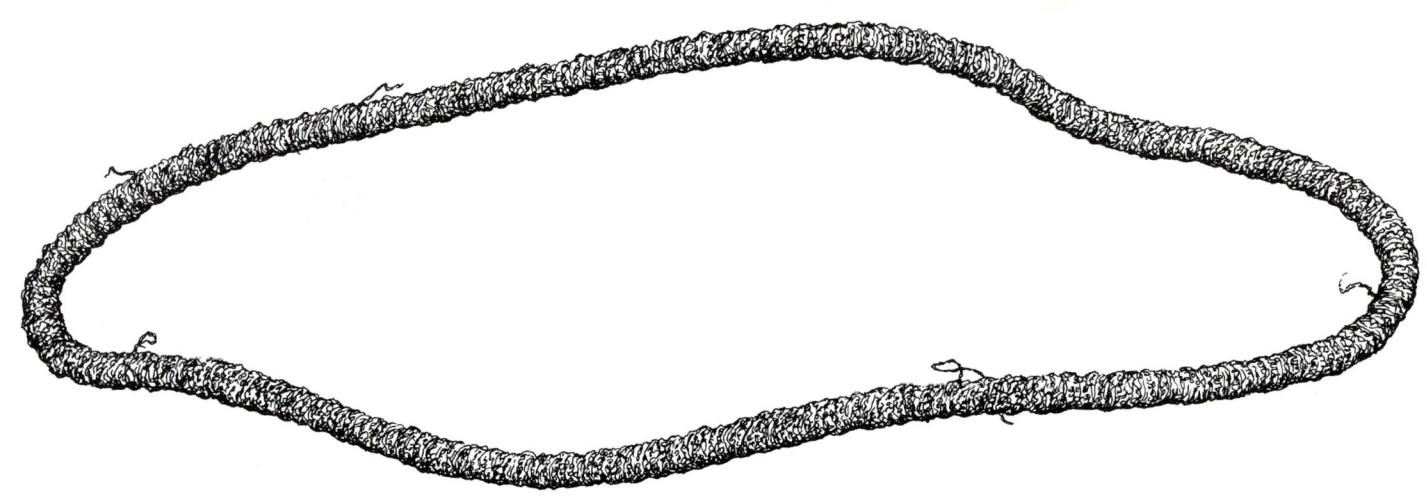

Above: A belt made from human hair

Below: The emu, a native Australian, grows to 5 or 6 feet tall. It can reach a top speed of 30 m.p.h.

flint which he would then glue to the shaft with *spinifex* resin. He could bind it with some of the kangaroo sinew that he always kept dangling from the belt of human hair at his waist. But the sun was well clear of the horizon and time valuable. They had far to travel before the *corroboree* that night. Sharpening and hardening the point in the embers would have to do. He went over to a rock of rough-grained sandstone and began to grind the spear against it, constantly turning the shaft in his hands. Quickly he had a sharp though rough point, which needed polishing if it were to slide through tough skin and flesh. As a carpenter uses finer and finer kinds of sandpaper when smoothing a piece of wood for furniture, Chimbani used less and less rough stones to grind down and polish the point. Finally the embers gave the last tempering. He tried the weight in his hand. The balance was good enough to kill a kangaroo or *emu* at seventy paces.

As the three walked back to camp, Chimbani tested the flight of the new weapon, seeing whether it veered to left or right, wobbled in flight or flew with the point or shaft too high in the air. In a while he was satisfied. Marbogwa

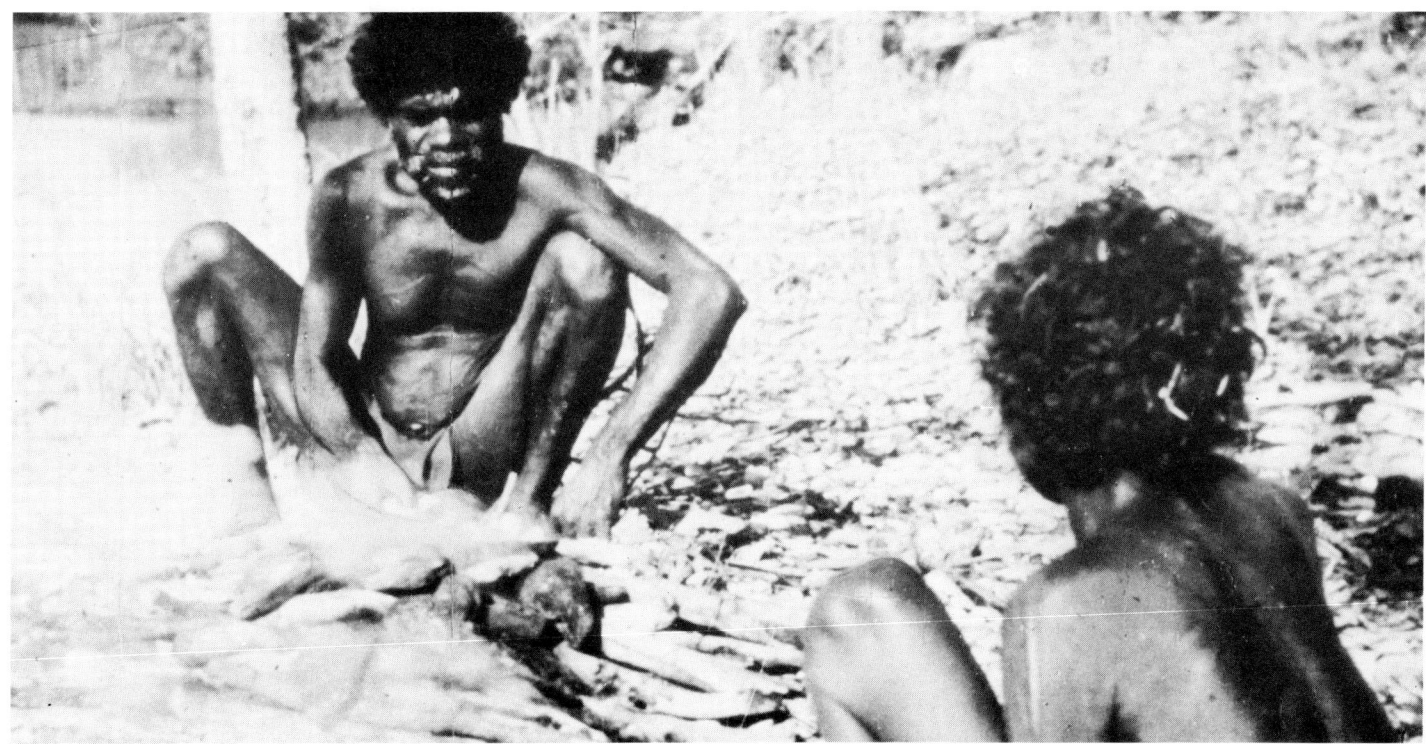

would have a spear to grace the arm of any hunter.

At the camp the goanna had been eaten, though a few choice pieces were kept for them. Wirri took the snake from Kinshari and tossed it on to the hot ashes. As the heat began to sear the skin, she turned it with a stick so that it would cook evenly. Then, after a very short time, she jerked it out, cooked on the surface only. Marbogwa divided the snake into three and gave the pieces to Chimbani, Bimba and Kinshari. As they ate, the blood dribbled down their chins and soon only the skull and backbone of the snake were left, which were crunched up by their *dingo*. Nothing remained; every part had been used – even the grease, which they carefully rubbed into their hair.

Now it was time to begin the day's march. As the desert *Aborigines* have few possessions, breaking camp did not take long. On the coldest of nights a rough windbreak of brushwood serves as shelter; for blankets, a hollow scooped in the ground or the ashes of a fire must do. Also, they had no cooking pots. The Aborigines never learnt the use of

Above: Two Aborigines (from northern Australia) wait by the fire for their dinner to cook. **Below:** A dingo. Many have been domesticated by the Aborigines

One of the few possessions of the native, the 'pointing bone' is used by some Aborigines to produce death-dealing spells on their enemies

clay, and the only containers they use are rough wooden bowls, mainly for carrying water to a camp or for gathering fruit, berries and seeds. They wander the territory of their family or tribal group with only the things they can tuck into a belt of human hair about the waist, which they keep supple and strong with emu fat or *ochre*. Otherwise, possessions must be held in the hand, while the women carry heavier things on a pad on their heads.

Some things are always left behind at a camp-site: stone tools that have been cracked by the sudden changes in temperatures, from the heat of day to the frosts of the night, and those selected only for temporary use, as Chimbani had done for severing the tjawu root. Then the women leave behind the heavy stones used for grinding *nardu* seeds. These come from a chocolate-brown, fern-like plant, and give a flour that is made into paste and then baked. They could not carry many things, and besides, in time they will return to the same place and the grinding stones will be used again. No other passing Aborigine would think of taking them away. So they take only their most valued possessions with them in their continuous forage for seasonal plant food. All possessions are a burden that hinders movement and reduces considerably the distance they can travel.

So they were equipped thus for the thirty-mile journey over the Gibson Desert to the corroboree at dusk. They carried no food or water. They had eaten better than they expected that morning, but on nothing choice enough to be worth *jerking*. If Marbogwa had brought in a kangaroo or emu they would still perhaps have eaten all of it, in much the same way as a camel drinks huge quantities of water and then continues for several days without more. As they had only wooden bowls they could carry little water, and much of that would be lost by an occasional stumble along the way.

They would not be worried by lacking either of these. The hunter might have no success with larger game during a day, but even the youngest child could catch a lizard to eat if he were hungry, or play with it and tear it to pieces if he were not. There were insects and grubs to be found also, including, with luck, the much sought-after *locust*.

In a dead landscape, that could be endured by a European only for a very few weeks after a drought had broken, they know, with the inherited knowledge of generations, where water can be found. Often it will not be visible and there will be no animal tracks or circling birds to guide them. But the Aborigine knows where to dig down a few feet through a dust-dry creek bed and come to water. It may be muddied, salt or sulphurous, or stained by copper or iron, but his stomach can accept it.

So the goods had been divided up. The women took the most, and the children a share. Marbogwa, hunter of the group, carried the tools of his trade: two spears, his spearthrower and a throwing stick. This was not a *boomerang*. Few adult Aborigines use a boomerang, for something that will fly straight is more valuable than the convenience of having a weapon return. They are mainly toys for children, or for sale in the far-off curio shops of Adelaide, Melbourne, Sydney and Perth. They are sent there by the mission stations around which many Aborigines have come to cluster in recent years for the benefits of civilisation – medicine, tobacco and a less formidable way of life.

Above: The influence of the white missionary on the Aborigine is shown in this picture of a priest with two native women in European dress, admiring an Aboriginal Madonna and Child in the Roman Catholic Cathedral, Darwin (northern Australia)

Below left: Two examples of the returning boomerang

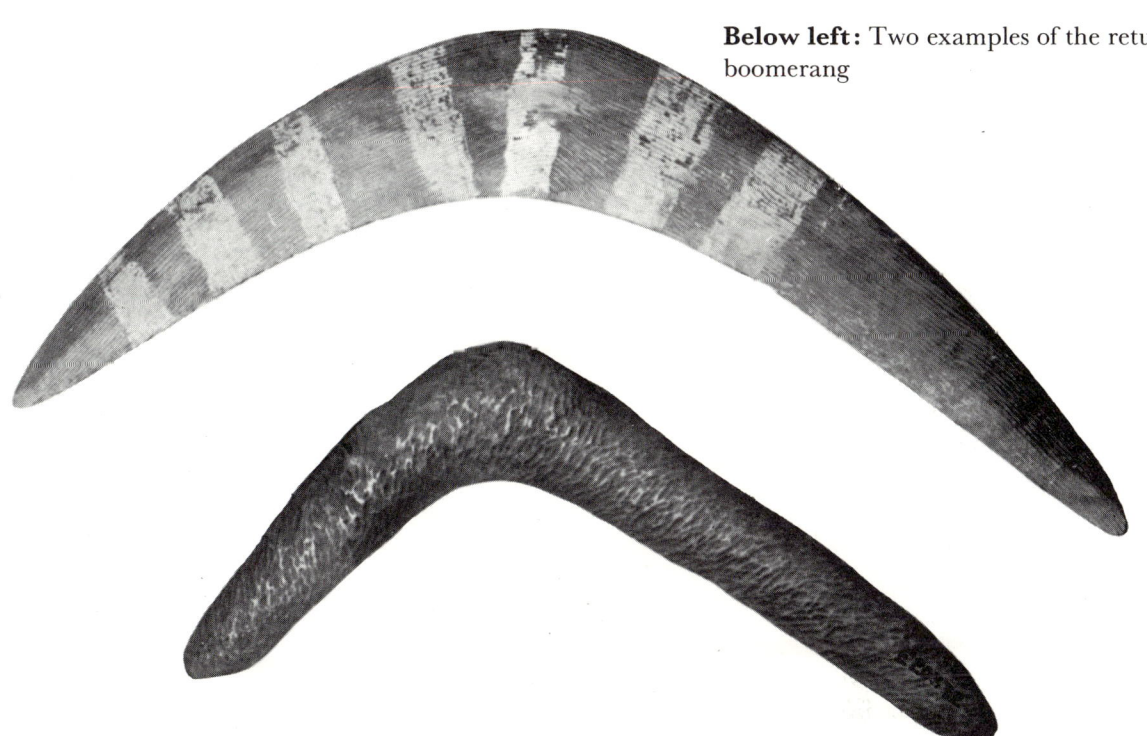

17

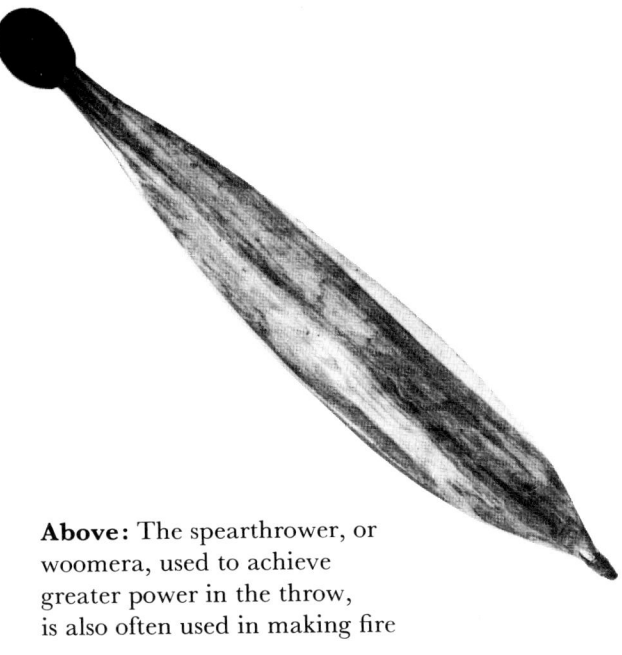

Above: The spearthrower, or woomera, used to achieve greater power in the throw, is also often used in making fire

A richly decorated shield from Western Australia

So Marbogwa's throwing stick was not right-angled like a boomerang. It was about eighteen inches long and curved at the end opposite to the grip, so that it would fly through the air more truly from an overarm throw. His spearthrower was a little less than three feet long and four inches wide, and was decorated with simple geometric carved designs. At one end was a lump of spinifex resin to prevent its slipping from his hand in use, and at the other a small bone hook to fit the notch in the shaft of his spear. It makes throwing a spear far more difficult, for the hook can slip out with the sudden force of a throw or, worse, a weak shaft may snap because of the extra power in a throw. But, with skill, the hunter can achieve more distance and penetration.

Although today used only by the Australian Aborigine, their use was once widespread in both Europe and North America. Illustrations of them have survived from ancient Egypt and the Sudan, while more recently they were used by the *Eskimo,* the *Aztec* and some of the North American 'Red' Indians. Most abandoned the spearthrower for the bow and arrow, but the Aborigines are a people who distrust change. Knowledge of the bow came to them from what is now Indonesia but they have never accepted it. Instead, like the boomerang, it became a toy for children.

Marbogwa's spearthrower had other uses. Set in a lump of resin was a skilfully-shaped *shard* of quartz. This he used mainly in woodworking for shaping the shaft of a spear, to carve other wooden things for decoration, or as a cutting edge and a piercer. Sometimes the curved upper surface of the thrower would be used as a kind of mixing bowl for paint, glue and food, or as a simple drum to accompany a tribal song. The spearthrower is used for just about everything.

With these implements in his hands, and a few strands of kangaroo sinew in his belt, Marbogwa moved off. Accompanied by Chimbani, he would travel ahead of the women and children, so that there would be time for hunting. He did not wish to arrive at the corroboree with no contribution to make to the feast.

Natanya, the old woman Anfrani and the children, were also ready. Wirri carried a smouldering hardwood stick that would save much of the trouble of making a fire if she kept it glowing through the day. The others carried wooden bowls that, if they were lucky in the empty wastelands, might be filled with berries and other desert fruit by the day's end. There were also the stone tools that had been made with care and were worth keeping: a hand-axe about six inches long and four inches wide, tapering to a point and with fine cutting edges. These were formed by first flaking away the flint from both sides and then polishing on a grindstone. Only the end that was to fit into the palm of the hand had no edge and, in fact, had been rounded off for comfort. There were other tools for working wood and cutting skin, and tools for special jobs. But the hand-axe served for many of the tasks of their everyday life. For those needing a specially keen edge, though, a stone knife was used. This was made from one of a number of suitable materials: chert, quartz, flint, obsidian or *volcanic glass*. A flake is struck off the core of these hard, brittle stones, and tiny slivers are then forced off the edge of the flake by pressing down firmly with a hardwood stick, or by tapping the stick with a hammer stone. Sometimes the teeth are used instead. When the knife is ready for use, it can be held in the hand with the forefinger along the back which will have been chipped blunt, or fitted into a piece of hardwood and fixed and bound with resin and a strip of leather or sinew. So this stone knife was also carried with them.

Breakfast had taken longer than usual, so the day's trek did not begin until late, at six o'clock. Already it was hot, but the temperature would soon climb far above the 100° of that hour. The Aborigine wastes little effort in the heat; his long legs move over the ground almost as though gliding and his flat feet do not sink into soft ground at the heel as a European's would.

As Natanya and Anfrani walked on steadily, the children wandered from side to side, darting off to examine the tracks of desert creatures that had passed this way. The two dingoes were glad to be on the move again but, because they had received a share of the morning's snake and goanna, they were hunting in play rather than with the thought of a kill.

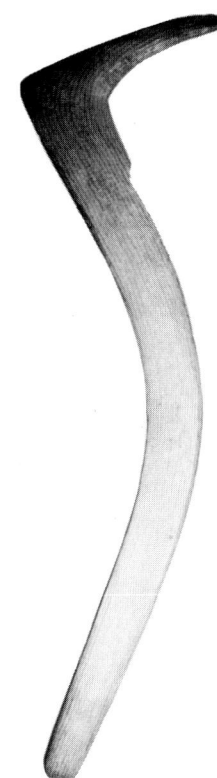

The throwing stick shown above was once used for throwing at enemies during tribal warfare

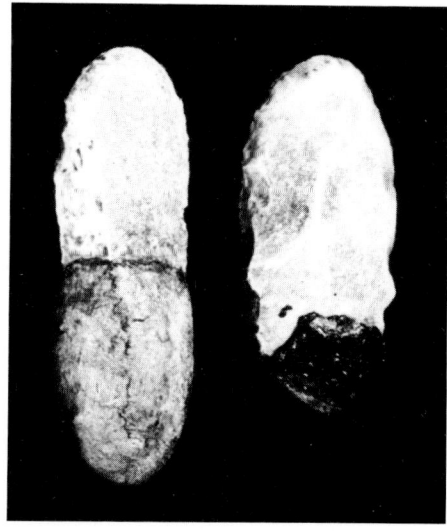

Two examples of Aboriginal stone knives with quartz blades

Above: Quandongs (*Santalum acuminatum*), which grow in the Gibson Desert, have soft green foliage and a large red or purple edible fruit which is said to have a similar taste to 'stewed plums'

Opposite: Sandstorms can arise suddenly and unexpectedly in an area such as the Gibson Desert; the conditions that result are a severe hindrance to travel

After an hour, both the dogs and the children settled to the long march. The heat had drained their high spirits but even the youngest, Kinshari and Bimba, knew that they must walk without complaint through the day. They could only expect to be carried if they were ill.

As the women walked, they constantly searched with experienced eyes for the bushes that carry edible berries and fruit. Although they were in desert country there had been rain a few weeks before, sufficient to bring life to dead bushes and seeds dormant beneath the ground. Even without rain, the water that often lies a few feet below a creek bed will keep a twisted bush or tree alive, when it appears to be dry and dead. After a couple of hours, Natanya paused in crossing a dry creek bed and turned to Anfrani, 'There is *ngaru* here!' Anfrani followed her pointing finger and nodded in agreement.

They sent the children on ahead, confident that they could find their tracks, even after a sudden sandstorm, and turned along the creek bed to a group of low bushes in a hollow. The bushes were still green because the hollow would have nurtured a pool for a week or two after the rain waters had seeped away into the sandy ground about it. It seemed dry, but probably still held moisture a few feet beneath the surface. Quickly they began to pick the ngaru. The ripe ones were like tiny green tomatoes. Most however had dried out in the sun, but too quickly to go rotten. They picked both kinds eagerly, for the fruit was as valuable dry as fresh. In a few minutes several pounds were in their bowls. Then they stopped. If they picked them all that day none would be left if they should pass that way again, and the ngaru stays edible on the bush for months. So they left some of the crop untouched.

Before following on after the children, Anfrani scooped the sand away at the lowest part of the hollow, and Natanya loosened it with her digging stick. At three feet down it began to get damp, then moist, and at six feet they came to water, warm and stained a chocolate brown. They drank, pausing frequently to spit out as much of the grit and sand as they could, but still swallowing a good deal. When they had satisfied their thirst, they filled one of their two remaining bowls with water and waited while

20

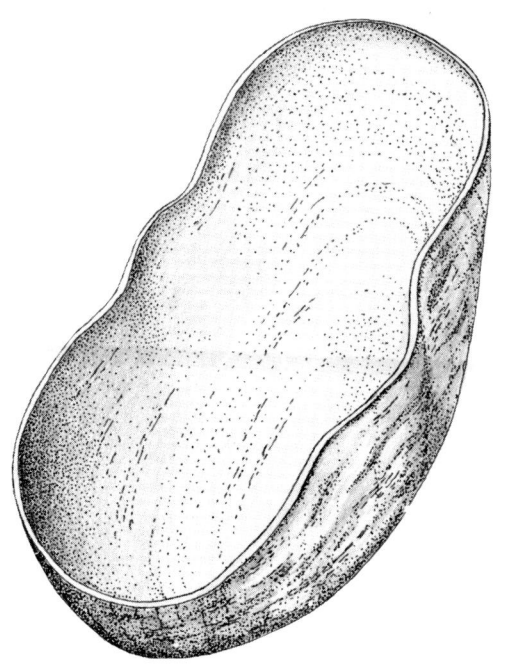

Above: A wallaby. **Below:** A wooden bowl used for carrying water, food and even babies

the sand settled at the bottom. Then they poured off the now lighter coloured water into the other bowl, and repeated this twice more until they were ready to move on with one full bowl of almost clear water. The final bowl they kept for the fruit, berries or seeds which they might yet find before they sheltered from the full heat of the sun.

When they caught up with the children again, they were walking wearily but no less steadily than before. Bimba was moving more heavily than the others, because of a burn on the sole of his foot from the hot ashes he had lain by the night before. He winced with each step but did not complain. Anfrani and Natanya gave each child a few ngaru. The dogs whined for water, but they would have to wait.

Marbogwa and Chimbani had earlier stopped at the same creek bed. Both had spotted the claw marks of an emu. They agreed that the tracks were three days old and not worth following, but the bird might have been on its way to water somewhere lower down the creek. If there was surface water, there was a chance of catching something by surprise.

After some time they began to pick out not only the tracks of their emu but also those of kangaroo, *wallaby* and lizards. It looked as if they must be approaching a favoured drinking place, for the tracks were now slanting down the shallow creek banks from every direction. Water could be the only reason for so many animals to pass this way. A patch of good grazing in the creek bottom would not have attracted the variety of creatures whose tracks they identified as they passed.

They began to move now without talking, holding their weapons so that they did not rattle one against another. The human smell would have frightened off any creatures down-wind of them, but they did not want any others that might be nearby to run, jump or slither away into the empty landscape.

Rounding a bend in the creek they saw the glint of water and stopped. A kangaroo stood drinking, perhaps two hundred yards off. With no words or sign being needed, they decided not to try for it. The kangaroo was alert, constantly stretching up on its long back legs and looking about it. It had possibly caught a scent of them, and was ready for flight. Marbogwa and Chimbani retreated round the bend and on further to a safe distance. If the kangaroo fled, other creatures would not venture to the water. They would wait, hoping it would come their way after it had drunk and that other creatures might pass the hiding place they had chosen.

They left the bed of the creek and scooped a hollow in the drifted sand, deep enough to keep them from sight when they lay down. Soon Chimbani was peering over the edge, on watch. Time passed, the sun hotter with every minute, and no breath of wind reaching into the hollow. To pass the time Chimbani improved the edge of a quartz spearpoint. Though a sharp point will penetrate the dense coat and tough skin of a kangaroo, the keenness of the edge is important too if the spear is to slide deep enough through the flesh to kill. He used his teeth to take off some fine slivers.

Then Chimbani gave a sign that something was moving. Quietly Marbogwa fitted his spear to the hook on his spearthrower, his hand sliding up to grip the grooves carved

The kangaroo (shown above) and the wallaby are abundant throughout Australia. They hop on their hind legs with the aid of a strong tail, and bounds of up to 25 feet at speeds of more than 25 m.p.h. have been reported. The young, called Joeys, are only about one inch long when born, and are suckled in a large pouch in the mother's body

in it. He touched Chimbani, and signed to him to keep down. Marbogwa would trust to his ears until whatever it was drew level with them along the creek bed below.

At last the moment arrived. Marbogwa rose to his feet and his arm swung back. The spear flew fast, straight and unwavering, the point a little high in the air. The emu turned quickly enough for its thigh bone to take the spearpoint, which then skidded across the bird's back, clattered over some rocks and sank into the creek bank on the other side. Already the bird was gone. In a few seconds its high-stepping, 30-m.p.h. gait had carried it out of range of a second spear.

The Aborigine hunter must at least wound with his first throw, to slow his *quarry* enough for a finishing attempt but, for Marbogwa and Chimbani the hours of waiting were to no avail. There would be no more hunting in this

Left: Two Aborigines well prepared for their hunting with spear, woomera, throwing stick and boomerang

place that day. Though there had been little noise, the wildlife would have been disturbed by the atmosphere of danger. Marbogwa and Chimbani followed on quickly after the women and children.

So the morning passed for this family as many other mornings had for their ancestors throughout the thousands of years since man first landed on the northern coast of Australia. The sun stood at its full height, yet the pace of the group did not waver. There was no talking. Strength was reserved for the business of walking and reaching the end of their journey. Soon, however, they must seek shade for a while, until the piercing strength of the hot sun lessened on its downward path towards the horizon.

Above: Coastal Aborigines also make use of the woomera in hunting. **Right:** Two successful hunters

AFTERNOON

Through the miles they had walked that day the land had changed little. There was the same pattern of stony desert, drifted dunes, dry creeks, a few trees and bushes tortured into strange shapes by thirst and the prevailing winds. Now at last the landscape changed. There was an upward slope towards an outcrop of sandstone rocks, rising from a sea of silver quartz sand that dazzled the eye and caused them to peer ahead through nearly shut eyelids. The walking was harder now as the fine sand gave beneath their feet at each step. Marbogwa, who had rejoined them some time before, pointed the way ahead. 'Through the gap,' he guided.

Through the layers of weathered sandstone was a track, carved out by some river thousands of years before the land grew dry. Now the sandy bottom of the gorge was as arid as the dunes that had been piled by the winds against the bare rocks. As they entered the gorge, the cliffs that rose on either side gave protection from the sun but in the

Above: Sandhills near Lake Carnegie, Gibson Desert

Right: By making use of rock shelters such as the one shown here, many Aborigines in the Gibson Desert gain protection from the fierce heat of the sun and the cold of the night

enclosed space it was even hotter. Marbogwa said, 'We must stop here awhile.'

The children threw themselves down on the sand which, out of the sun, no longer stung them, although in the unshaded desert its sharp heat had penetrated even the thick toughened skin of their feet. The others came up and Chimbani pointed above, 'There's a better place up there. I remember water there when I was a boy.' He was pointing at a cave some fifty feet above the floor of the gorge. The silt and sand, left behind by the occasional flash flood that roared through the gorge, formed an easy slope up to the entrance. They climbed up, although no one believed that there would still be water seeping into the cave through the sandstone after the weeks that had passed since the last of the rains.

The children were the first to reach the cave, delighted by the sudden chill of the air as they stooped low to enter it. Though there was no sound of water, the cool dampness of the air felt good on their dried, sun-scorched skin. Once they were inside, the cave opened out into a cavern

Above: Looking north across the Gibson desert

A north-eastern view of the Rawlinson Range, in the Gibson Desert

27

Above: Aboriginal rock paintings

Below: Handprints left by Aborigines on a cave wall

Opposite: Bimba helps Marbogwa make a handprint inside the cave

scoured out of the sandstone by thousands of years of seeping and flowing water. All over the low dome-like roof, from the floor of the cave to the highest part, were hundreds of drawings and paintings. Bimba turned to Barrimba and asked his brother what they were. He replied, 'They were made I think many years ago. In the *Dreamtime*. But our father sometimes does work something like them.' By now Marbogwa and the others had followed their children into the cave. He smiled to see them running about, pausing to look more closely at a drawing from time to time, before going on to another. It was all a wonder. None of them had seen anything quite like it, though they had seen drawing in the sand, on rocks and in caves often before.

Marbogwa called the children to him. 'It is time for you to know more of such things. I will tell you what they are and how they are made.' He pointed first at a part of the roof which had a large number of outlines of human hands. 'That is something any of you can do. I think we may find some paint left by other people.'

He looked closely around the floor of the cave, his eyes now becoming used to the dimness after the dazzle of the reflecting sands outside, and the shimmering of the open plain. At several places on the cave floor he noticed small shallow holes worn in the sandstone. He went over to one of them and gestured to Anfrani to bring a wooden bowl. Bending down, he picked out a piece of burnt wood. 'Charcoal,' he said, crushing it between his fingers into the palm of his hand. He walked over to where the curve of the roof met the floor, and smeared a small area of the rock with spittle. 'Bimba, come here.' He took the boy's hand and placed it against the roof, fingers spread. 'Hold it there without moving.' Marbogwa then held up the hand with the powdered charcoal in, and blew the dust gently and evenly over his son's hand and on to the wall behind it. Bimba took his hand away when told to do so, leaving the outline behind. It was very like all the others on the roof, if a little smaller.

'Father, that was so easy,' said Barrimba, 'I have heard people say that you know the secret of these things, but what you have done is nothing special. And why put the

Above: Many Aboriginal rock paintings are connected with myth and magic. This painting, found in North Australia, shows the Lightning Brothers, mythical beings associated with the perpetuation of rain. Whenever their colours begin to fade they are ceremonially repainted according to ancient tribal custom

Below: The ancient Asian technique of brass and stone rubbing has been used here to copy a rock-carving depicting two Aborigines

sign of a hand in a cave?' Marbogwa wondered for a moment if he should show anger. But he decided he was pleased his son was not afraid to speak what he felt. 'What I have done is for the young and the elderly who are not capable of more,' he said. 'Later I shall show you more difficult things. I do not know why so many of our people have left the sign of their hands here, but there are many things that no man knows.'

If Marbogwa had seen a *Byzantine* church in Libya, a Roman fort in Syria, a medieval castle in England, or even a school desk, he would have noticed the same thing. Human beings have an instinct to leave behind them signs that they have been to a place, have been alive and are not nothing. The outlines of hands left by *Cro-Magnon* man in the caves of France and Spain, by the *Bushmen* in the *Kalahari Desert*, by unknown peoples in the *Tassili N'Ajjer* mountains of Algeria and by the Australian Aborigines, come from the same human desire not to be entirely forgotten, as does a name cut into a tree or the stone of a castle battlement today.

Marbogwa led the children about the cave, pointing at many of the drawings above their heads and explaining what some of them meant. He spoke first of a design of circles and straight lines. 'That is the journey of a father of our people many years ago, in the Dreamtime. It shows his journey through this country when our people first came here. The circles are water-holes, and the lines mark the way he went from one to another. And what is that one?' It was a very simple design – a solid line with two dotted lines running along at either side. Barrimba said, 'A mother with her children.'

'No', said Marbogwa, 'It is a kind of magic. Hunters even now after so many years still wait here for animals to come by and they throw their spears down at them as they go past. If you draw the animal on the rock, or show his tracks, it makes him come more quickly. That one is for a goanna. This middle line is the mark his belly makes in the sand, and the others are the marks of his feet. And this one?' He was smiling now, remembering the hunting that same day. It was the arrow-like tracks left by an emu. 'Kangaroo!' Barrimba called out, interrupting. This time no one was in doubt. The artist had painted the form of the animal itself and not a symbol of it. The kangaroo had been caught perfectly, rising on its rear legs, head half turned listening and looking. Strangely, the inside of the animal was shown as well – the parts where a spear might kill it, the best pieces to eat, spine, heart, liver, stomach.

Marbogwa decided that he had talked enough, and that he would show them how a painting is done. He looked about the cave floor for materials left behind by others, from which he could make his colours. Black was easy. Charcoal from many old fires littered the floor. For white he would use pipeclay, or the rarer white ochre. Red he got from a lump of ochre. He put this in one of the holes which would act as a *mortar*, and used the shaft of his spear for a *pestle*. Quickly he ground enough for his needs to a fine powder, but he had to fix his paint, still dust, to the rock where it should last as long as the other works. He was famous as a painter among his people, and he wanted his work to last. So to bind the dust he mixed in emu fat, and the juice of the ngaru which the women

Rock-carving of a wallaby, New South Wales. The carving is actually life-size and would have been cut to the depth of an inch with sharpened stones, many years before the white people arrived in Australia

had picked that morning. A twig, chewed vigorously at one end so that the wood fibres separated, became his brush. At times he would use his finger, too, for lines of a different quality.

He began to draw in sweeping curves. Quickly an emu took shape and, remembering the morning's failure, there were some magic symbols too. A few lines in black showed two men hunting the bird. One watched; the other was stooping forward after throwing his spear. The spear was safely in the bird's heart. The success of these hunters was what Marbogwa hoped would befall him, the next time he went out to kill an emu.

There was half of their journey yet ahead of them and, although the temperature was still 120°, the fire of the day's heat was ebbing. They must move on. They left the cave after sharing out the water Natanya had carried since the ngaru gathering, and continued along the gorge.

Once they had left it, the sandstone hills gave way to the same kind of country that they saw every day of their lives – brush, stony desert, dried-up water courses, drifted sand. A warm wind rose. Beginning as a breath on the skin, it was soon blowing strongly, carrying the fine sand that can penetrate any building, and that can be kept out of nose and eyes only by clothing that masks the face – the Arab *burnous* for example, or blanket-like clothing that can muffle the face when need be. The Aborigines' clothing gave them little protection. There were no rocks nearby to fend off the full force of the storm, which had now risen to a peak, blasting their skin with grit and whipping small sharp stones up against their legs.

In one way they were fortunate. The wind was not in their faces. It blew from behind, helping them on their way, only occasionally forcing them to the ground with its power. Their eyes could still see, shielded from the full force. As the storm rose, the sun became only a blood-red glint through the haze of dust and sand that now soared thousands of feet upwards. But this was not a bad storm; after little more than an hour the wind began to drop, and they came from the darkness into sunlight again. Such winds can blow for days from one direction and when

Above: Two Aborigine hunters from the Great Sandy Desert

Below: An Arab burnous worn over the face

Opposite page: Cave painting of a woman with fish – from the Northern Territory

Above: A typical water-hole which the desert Aborigines would make for on their travels

relief seems to be on its way, can turn and blow as long from the other. In the end, even the most hardened Aborigine may lie down and die, unable to see or find food and water, exhausted by the unceasing attack of wind, heat, dust and sand.

In the darkness, swept on by the wind, they had moved fast, continuing the rhythm of their smooth strides. The sacred water-hole where the corroboree was to be held now lay only a few miles off.

As always they scanned the ground for tracks as they walked on, without a pause in step. The end of their journey was nearer and they began to notice traces on the bare plain, which showed that others had come that way. In the distance smoke rose. They began to quicken their strides; the children with new energy darted off again from their route in pursuit of lizard tracks. Marbogwa became more alert, hoping he might still hunt down something larger than this. But there was little chance now. Men, besides the dingo the only carnivorous creatures in the Gibson Desert, had passed by, and the animals and birds that feared them were gone.

Right: An example of a more luxuriant water-hole

EVENING

Above: A gathering of natives watch the dancers in a corroboree

As the end of the day's journey grew nearer, the older ones began to think of the reason for their journey. Marbogwa's other wife, Nyalunga, had died of tuberculosis some three months before. They had sung to her as she died to comfort her on her journey to the sky, and had mourned her passing. She had been buried quickly and without ceremony, in a grave that was probably marked now only by a drift of sand pushing up against the low mound of her grave. Her body had been treated with this much respect, but it was really of no more interest. It was for the sake of her spirit that they had come to meet with the relatives at the corroboree. Ceremonies must be performed to make sure that her spirit was satisfied and would not return to trouble the living.

At the water-hole preparation had been under way all day. Marbogwa's group was the last to reach the place. Hanging from the sparse mulga bushes, or leaning against rocks, were a scattering of the presents that the relatives would exchange after the ceremonies. The dancers had already begun to prepare themselves. Marbogwa greeted

Below: The small tree surrounded by 'everlasting flowers' in the foreground is a mulga bush

35

The above photograph shows Aborigines from northern Australia in corroboree dress. The corroboree is an important event for the Aborigine as a means of social intercourse. Generally held for social-religious purposes, such as the initiation of young men, or, as here, the ritual mourning of the dead, it is also of economic importance, being an opportunity for trade and the exchange of ideas

them and looked at them closely to make sure that all had been done in accordance with custom. The decorations on their bodies followed patterns used for generations. Pipeclay lines were drawn across the forehead and cheekbones and down the nose; broad-banded lines swung from the centre of the breast up to the shoulders and along the arms; on their legs were the decorations they had seen in the cave that day, parallel lines linked to circles. All had spears, to defend against the evil spirits that would be faced and fought during the dance.

The musicians who would stir them on began to test their instruments, two only on this occasion. An old, old man, his skin dried out like the paper bark of a *eucalyptus* tree, whose eyes, nose and mouth seemed to be one with the deep lines of his face, was to drum. His drum was two lengths of hardwood which when struck gave out different notes. He would keep the rhythm of the dance, while the lungs of a younger man produced a long soaring wail from the *didjeridu*. This was a wooden tube some six feet long, broadening towards the end and quite similar to the horn still played in Switzerland, Scandinavia and Eastern Europe, or the trumpet of the *Iturbi* pygmies of the Congo.

Wirri and Barrimba had a part to play too. They had each been given a *bull-roarer*, an oval of wood about two feet long which, at a signal from the player of the didjeridu, they began to whirl around their heads with a leather thong. The air rushed over the bull-roarers as they whirled them faster and faster, and the whirring sound rose to a high-pitched whine. The sound is both a signal and a warning – a warning if a special corroboree is forbidden

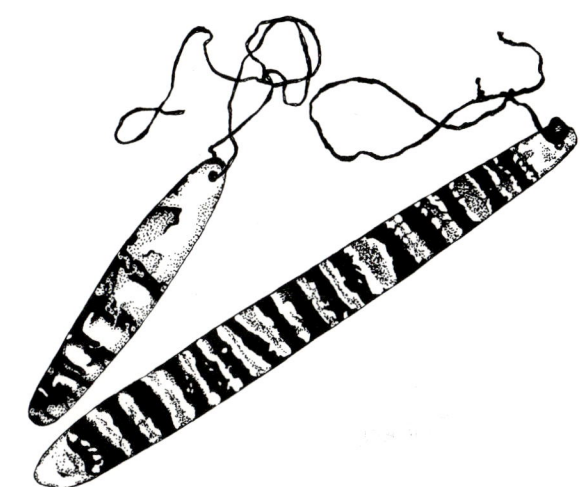

Above: Two examples of sacred bull-roarers. **Below:** An Aborigine plays the didjeridu, while his companion rhythmically clicks sticks

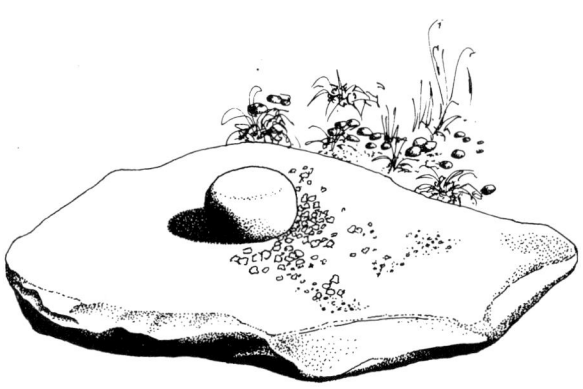

Above: Grinding stones are normally left at the camp-site as they are too bulky to be carried long distances

Below: Feathered head-dresses are common among the Aborigines of Central Australia

to women and uninitiated men, for if they wander unaware into such a ceremony they must be killed – but on this occasion it was a sign that all should gather, that dance and ceremony were now beginning.

The children withdrew and Marbogwa and Natanya came into the circle formed by the dancers, she with a stone in her hand and he with a spear. The drums pounded urgently, and the tone of the didjeridu rose. Marbogwa gave a long echoing cry of despair and drew the edge of his spear-point across his forehead, and made jabbing movements against his chest and shoulders. Blood flowed. Natanya struck herself on cheek and breast with the stone, and scraped it down her arm. Their flowing blood was a sign that grief was deeply felt. Natanya cried out too and threw herself to the ground, beating her fists on the stony surface, and rubbing her face against it repeatedly. Marbogwa gashed himself in the arm and across the breast. The spirit of Nyalunga would see that she was not forgotten and that the mourning was genuine.

Chimbani brought the few possessions of the dead woman into the circle. He hurled a grinding stone against a rock again and again until it shattered. He then placed two wooden bowls, a hair belt and a piece of cloth in a hollow and, taking up a firestick, some dried grass and twigs, began to burn them. Aborigines do not use the possessions of anyone who has died. The evil spirit that caused the death may linger on in the things they used in life, and may come out to attack with sickness, accident or even death. But if these things are broken or burned, the spirits that live in them are destroyed, or at least will leave so uncomfortable a home.

Marbogwa and Natanya had now played out their part. Calm again, they left the circle. Chimbani remained, surrounded by the dancers who circled Nyalunga's smouldering possessions, chanting rhythmically, and in turn began to stamp on the ashes. As they did so, the evil spirits left Nyalunga's possessions and began to pass one by one into the squatting Chimbani. Shaking with new burdens as each entered, he rose to his feet and began to move in time with the dancers, his body and face twisted in pain and suffering. The lead dancer came up to him and

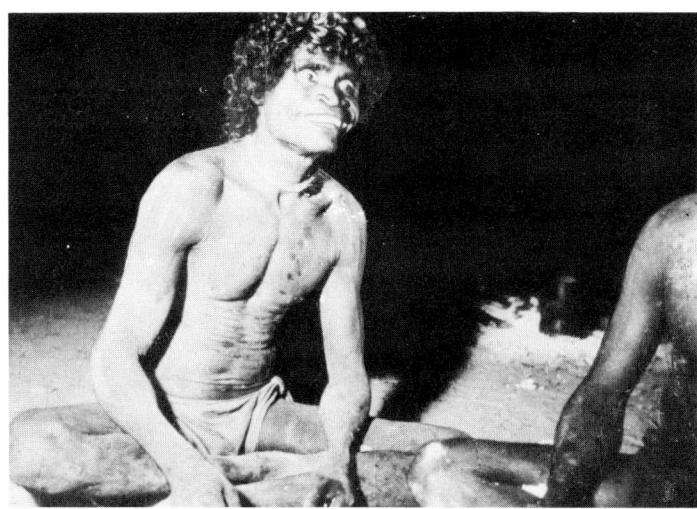

began to pluck the spirits from him – from ears, nose and mouth. Each time he cried out in triumph, and his bearing increasingly showed contempt as he tossed a defeated spirit away from him. The music of the didjeridu seemed to echo his success and became gayer and more lilting. The old man straightened, and the pain left his face. He joined the dancers. All began to chase the spirits, that had fled from Chimbani's body, away from the gathering. Their defeat was now complete. The dance became joyous, a celebration that the task had been finished and that there was nothing to fear any longer.

Marbogwa and Natanya rejoined the group. The cycle of mourning for Nyalunga was complete. All now revolved round the didjeridu player and the dancing reflected the fact that the corroboree was no longer a mourning of death, but a celebration of triumph over forces of evil. Nyalunga was now of the past, her spirit happy in the sky.

In time the liveliness of the didjeridu and the pace of the dance lessened, as the strength of both dancers and the player ebbed. It was replaced by quieter rhythms and emotions. Eventually, after a final long drawn-out note, the air was still. It was time for eating and the exchange of gifts among the relatives of Nyalunga.

Though Marbogwa's hunting that day had not gone well, others had been more successful. There were young kangaroos, desert pheasant, parrots, a dingo, plenty of fat grubs and locusts. Marbogwa's brother, who lived many miles away on the edge of the desert, by a creek that held

Above left: A northern bush Aborigine tells a story by the camp fire.
Above: The pale-headed rosella, a native parrot, eats the seeds of a Blackboy tree

water almost all the year round, had proudly brought three wild ducks which he had killed with a borrowed gun. Natanya had the fruit she had picked that morning, and the other women had also brought fruit and berries. There was plenty of nardu flour to bake cakes in the hot ashes, for those that were still not full when the meat was finished. Because the Aborigine eats hugely when there is food in plenty, there would be none left by the time they were ready for sleep. The children learn this lesson very young, and they eat nearly as much as the adults.

As they sat eating, the successful hunters of the day selected the choicest pieces of the creatures they had killed for their relatives, and ate the less favoured parts themselves. They were compensated, though, by getting the best pieces from their fellow hunters' catch.

When the didjeridu player had eaten, the music began again. This time there was no frenzy in his playing. As the moon rose higher and they circled the fire more closely

The flesh-cutting ceremony is an endurance test which all young male Aborigines must undergo. The flesh is cut with a sharp flint and pepper is rubbed in. The young man must not make any sound, so to prevent an involuntary cry he holds a wooden ball between his teeth

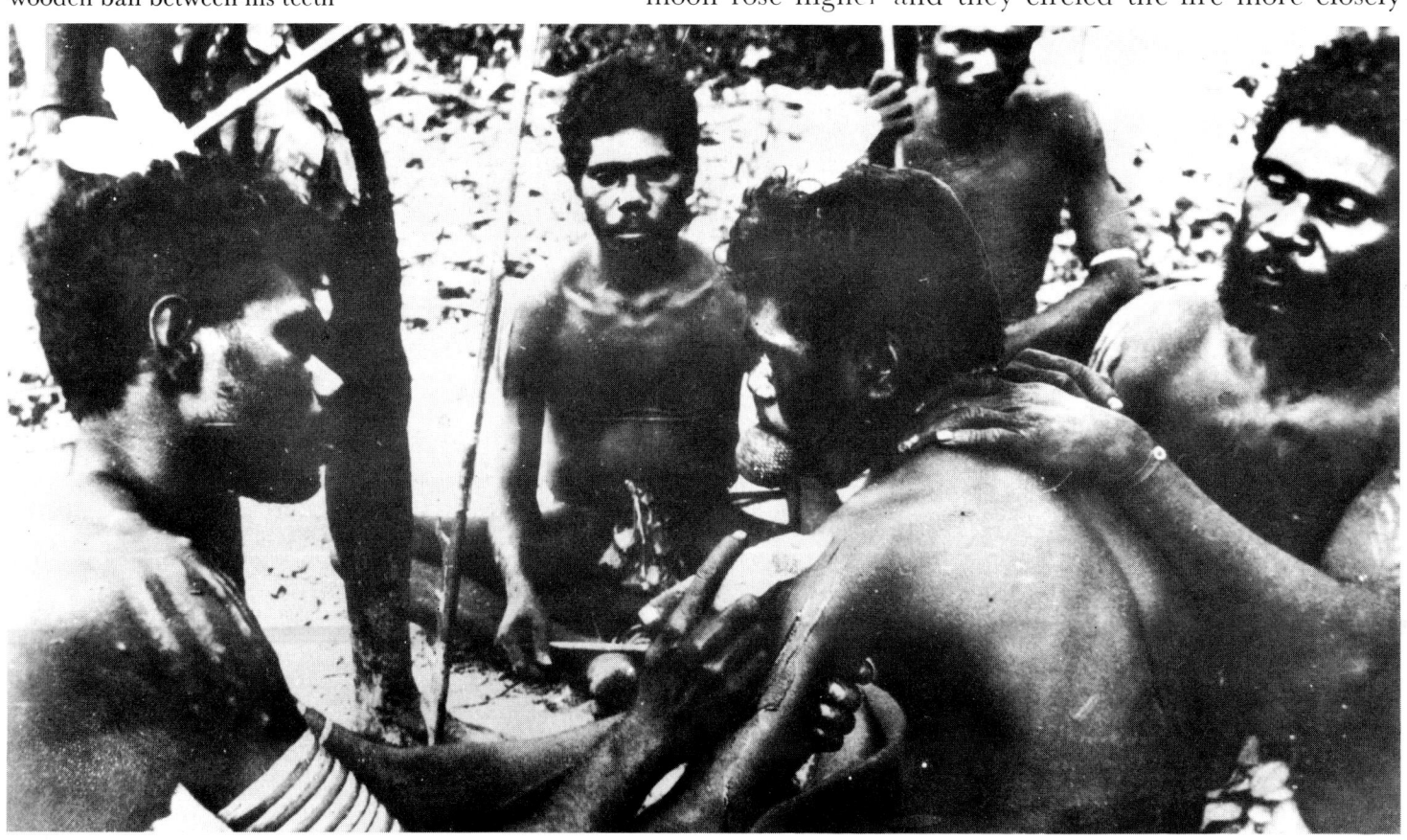

against the night chill, the traditional songs of their people were sung. The songs told of the coming of the white man to their lands, with his guns and sheep, and of the strange curses that had then fallen on the Aborigine – how many had begun to cough and grow thin, and how much of their country had become empty of people, as young and old had died. They told of sudden and frightening fevers that sometimes emptied an encampment in a day. They sang too of their spirit ancestors who had first travelled the length of Australia in the Dreamtime, of the beauty of the women, and of hunters whose skill and daring had won lasting fame. The songs died away, and they began to tell each other of the lives they would return to now that Nyalunga's death had been honoured.

The old way of life passed away more quickly and finally with each year. None gathered round the fire lived the same life as their forefathers. For all of them, the journey to the

Above: The white man brought many strange things with him
Below: Aboriginal and white stockmen work together in the outback

corroboree had been a return to the old ways. Tomorrow they would return to the world of railways, clothes, huts and tinned food. For many of the men it would be to remote sheep or cattle stations where they would ride, the cowboys of Australia, over the long miles, finding a new but different pride of achievement, in raising the animals that are so great a part of the country's livelihood. Some would return to lonely Christian missions where they would hear talk of a different god, receive food and clothing and in return make things, with the craft of their people, that could be sold.

Nevertheless times would come again when they must leave the white man's life, leave his huts and take off his clothes, forfeit his tobacco and flour and go back to the empty lands where their race had grown old before the rule of the Pharaohs.

In a while the place grew still and the fire dulled under the brilliance of the moon. The Aborigines slept.

Evidence of the white man's mark on many parts of inland Australia, this government bore in the Northern Territory is of enormous importance in the rearing of cattle

Glossary

aborigine	a person who has lived in a country from the earliest time
Aztec	Mexican Indian civilization conquered by the Spanish adventurer, Cortes
boomerang	an Australian throwing stick that returns to the thrower
bull-roarer	a piece of wood which, when swung, gives out a note. Common in England until 18th century
burnous	a hooded cloak worn particularly by North African Arabs and Berbers
Bushmen	a people living in the Kalahari Desert of southern Africa
Byzantine	to do with Byzantium (now Constantinople) capital of the Eastern Roman Empire
chert	a form of quartz with a flinty appearance
corroboree	meeting and dance of Australian Aborigines
creek	a short arm of a river, usually without a noticeable current
Cro-Magnon	a race of people living in western Europe 20,000 years aso. First modern humans
didjeridu	Australian musical instrument made from wood
dingo	wild Australian dog, sometimes domesticated
Dreamtime	in Aboriginal beliefs, the time of the creation of the world
emu	a large Australian bird, related to the ostrich and cassowary
Eskimo	aboriginal of the Arctic regions
eucalyptus	a kind of gum tree mainly found in hot, dry, sandy conditions
firestick	a hardwood stick used in making fire
flash flood	a sudden rush of water after rain in dry or desert climates
flint	a hard, brittle stone composed of silica, much used for making stone tools
goanna	a large lizard, two species of which are found in the Gibson Desert. Both are hunted by the Aborigines for food
ironwood	a term for any very hard wood, and often used to denote the tjawu tree
Iturbi	a pygmy tribe
jerk	to cut meat into narrow strips and dry it in the sun to preserve it
Kalahari	desert of southern Africa
locust	a winged insect, rather like a grasshopper, which moves in swarms, devouring all vegetation
mortar	kind of bowl in which ingredients can be pounded to mix or grind
mulga	Australian bush
nardu	a kind of flour made by Aborigines from a fern-like Australian plant
ngaru	an Australian shrub, bearing a small tomato-like fruit which forms an important part of the Aborigine's diet
obsidian	a glass-like volcanic rock or lava
ochre	earth containing oxides of iron and used in the making of paint
pestle	tool for pounding materials in a mortar in order to grind or mix them
quarry	a creature pursued by a hunter
quartz	a mineral used for making stone tools and sometimes jewellery
shard	a fragment of stone or pottery
spearthrower	wooden device used by the Australian Aborigines to increase the force of a spear throw
spinifex	plant from which a natural resinous glue can be obtained
Tassili N'Ajjer	mountains of the interior of Algeria, famous for their prehistoric cave art

tjawu	a tree which grows in the Australian desert, one of the *Acacia* species. Often called 'ironwood' or 'gidgee'
totem	natural object, such as an animal, tree, etc., thought of as an emblem of a person or a clan; often symbolized in carvings on a pole or in rock
volcanic glass	a glass-like rock
wallaby	a small species of kangaroo
woomera	Australian wooden device to increase the force of a spear throw

General Notes

GENERAL BELIEFS

The Australian Aborigines believe that life on earth was created during a period known as the **Dreamtime**, when supernatural spirits came from the earth, the sea and the sky and took on the shapes of all forms of animal and plant life. When an Aborigine woman finds she is expecting a child, she believes that one of these spirits has planted that life in her and she looks around her for any sign of the spirit which has entered her body. She may see a lizard, a plant, a water-hole – whatever it is that she decides the spirit is in, becomes the personal **totem**, or emblem, of her child. Throughout his life, this totem will watch over him, protect him and warn him of any potential danger. In return he must respect his totem and fulfil various obligations towards it. If it is a type of animal, he must not eat that animal. This personal myth the Aborigine calls his **dreaming**.

SOCIAL RELATIONSHIPS

The desert Aborigines have a complex system of relationships which enables them to classify another person as soon as they meet him, and so to treat him immediately in the correct manner according to their very strict laws of etiquette between groups. Every man or woman belongs to one of four (or sometimes more) sections. These are of enormous importance to the Aborigine, particularly when it comes to marriage. A man belonging to one category (say, the **Panaka**) may only choose his wives from one other specified group (in this case, the **Tjaruru**). Their children would then be classified in a third group which, in turn, is obliged to marry into a specified fourth group. Failure to abide by these marriage rules can mean punishment of death.

The groups, however, do not in any way imply wealth or rank, and each group, commonly called a kinship group, has its own totem which must be respected and looked after in much the same way as each man's personal emblem. Throughout the world people find the need for some kind of social grouping.

THE TRIBE

Generally, the Aborigines tend to live in tribes, but in the desert they resort to scattered family groups which are called **myalls.** They are a generous people and expect to share the food that they gather. Equally, they expect to receive a share of what others may find.

Children are highly indulged when they are young and are seldom punished. However, when they reach puberty, they must begin to participate in the rigours of their society, undergoing various initiation rites and ceremonies until they become full members of their community. Tribal wars are relatively uncommon and these, as well as personal quarrels, are usually over a point of honour, which is settled when blood is drawn or when the injustice is paid for in some way. Men often have more than one wife, and jealousies among the wives of a particular husband may result in fighting. In these cases, the women resort to a strict form of duelling in which one woman will bend her head for the other to beat with a club. The two women take it in turns to beat each other in this way until one falls stunned to the ground.

CEREMONIES

Many types of ceremony take place among the Aborigines. Some are connected with the history of the tribe and its continuation. These involve the legend and lives of the spirit heroes of the Dreamtime and would include the **corroboree** held in this story for the expulsion of the spirits from Nyalunga's possessions. Other ceremonies are bound up with the totems of individuals, kinship groups and tribes, and are designed to ensure the continued prosperity and goodwill of the particular totem. Yet others exist merely for the purpose of telling stories and entertaining.

NOMADIC LIFE

The desert Aborigines have few possessions. To them possessions are often an unnecessary burden. Anything large that they own is usually left at a camp site for use on a future occasion. Small tools, wooden bowls, etc., they take with them as these are often needed on their travels.

They wander the desert, making instinctively for water-holes, and gathering food as they go. They hunt when they can but over half of their diet consists of vegetable foods, which ripen at varying times throughout the year. Meat is not easy to obtain, and emu and kangaroo form only a small percentage of the diet. Smaller game, and the lizard in particular, is a very much more important source of protein.

The greater reliance on vegetables than on meat results in some bodily deficiencies, especially among the children, who have a tendency to develop swollen stomachs. This condition generally disappears after a few years and is accepted by the people as something quite normal. Many Aborigines wear no clothes at all but many others wear a very simplified form of clothing something like a loin-cloth, or merely a hair belt. Some desert Aborigines wear a type of sandal (woven from plants) on their feet as a protection against the scorching sands of the desert.

For protection from the fierce heat of the day or cold of the night they sometimes construct simple rock or bush shelters.

Index

Adelaide, 17
Algeria, 30
Ancient Egypt, 18
Australia, 25, 41, 42
Aztec, 18

Blankets, 15
Boomerang, 17, 18
Bow, 18
Bowls, 16, 18, 19, 20, 28, 38
Bull-roarer, 37
Burial, 35
Burnous, 33
Bushmen, 30
Byzantine, 30

Camp, 10
Carrying pad, 16
Carving, 18
Caves, 27, 28, 30, 31, 33
Cave paintings and drawings, 28, 30,
    31, 33
Charcoal, 28, 31
Chert, 10, 19
Coming of the white man, 10, 41
Congo, the, 37
Corroboree, 14, 16, 18, 34, 35–42
Cowboys, 42
Crafts, 10, 42
Creek, 7, 11, 13, 17, 20, 22, 23, 24, 26
Cro-magnon man, 30

Dancing, 38, 39
Death, 35
Desert pheasant, 31
Didjeridu, 37, 38, 39, 40
Digging stick, 11, 20
Dingo, 15, 19, 34, 39
Dreamtime, 30, 41
Drought, 17
Drum, 18, 36, 37

Eastern Europe, 37
Emu, 14, 16, 22, 23, 24, 30, 31, 33
England, 30
Eskimo, 18

Eucalyptus, 36
Europe, 18
Evil spirits, 38, 39

Feet, 19
Fire, 8, 13, 19
Firestick, 8, 13, 38
Flash floods, 13, 27
Flint, 9, 10, 13, 19
Food and drink, 8, 9, 10, 12, 15, 16,
    17, 20, 39, 40
France, 30

Gibson Desert, 16, 34
Goanna, 8, 9, 15, 19, 30
Gorge, 26, 27, 33
Grinding stones, 16, 38
Gun, 40, 41

Hand-axe, 13, 19
Honour, 10
Human hair belt, 14, 16, 38
Hunter, 8, 16, 17, 30, 33, 41
Hunting, 12, 18, 19, 23, 24, 30, 33, 39

Indonesia, 18
Insects and grubs, 16, 39
Ironwood, 11, 12
Iturbi pygmies, 37

Jerking, 16

Kalahari Desert, 30
Kangaroo, 10, 14, 16, 18, 23, 30, 31,
    39

Libya, 30
Lizard, 8, 16, 23, 34
Locust, 16, 39

Magic, 30, 33
Medicine, 17
Medieval castle, 30
Melbourne, 17
Mission stations, 17, 42
Mortar, 31
Mulga, 8, 13, 35
Music, 36, 37, 38, 40

Musical instruments, 36, 37, 38

Nardu, 16, 40
Ngaru, 20, 22, 31
North America, 18

Obsidian, 10, 19
Ochre, 16, 31

Painting, 30, 31, 33
Parrots, 39
Perth, 17
Pestle, 31
Pharaohs, 42

Quarry, 24
Quartz, 18, 19, 23, 26

Red Indians, 18
Roman fort, 30

Sandstorm, 20, 33
Scandinavia, 37
Shard, 18
Silt, 27
Snake, 9, 11, 12, 15, 19
Song, 18, 41
Spain, 30
Spear, 10, 13, 14, 15, 17, 23, 24, 30,
    33, 36, 37
Spearshaft, 10, 11, 13, 14, 18, 31
Spearthrower, 8, 17, 18, 23
Spinifex, 14, 18
Stone knife, 19
Sudan, the, 18
Switzerland, 37
Sydney, 17
Syria, 30

Tassili N'Ajjer, 30
Temperature, 19, 33
Tempering wood, 13, 14
Throwing stick, 10, 17, 18
Tjawu, 11, 16
Tobacco, 17, 42
Tools, 8, 9, 10, 11, 13, 14, 16, 17, 18,
    19, 31
Totem, 10

Tracks, 9, 10, 11, 17, 19, 22, 23, 30, 34
Tribal fight, 10

Volcanic glass, 19

Wallaby, 23
Water, 16, 17, 23, 27, 33
Water-hole, 30, 34, 35
Weapons, 17, 23
Wild duck, 40
Winds, 9, 11, 26, 33, 34
Wives, 10
Woman's place, 8, 17
Woomera, 8, 10

Further Reading

The Original Australians   A. A. Abbie (Muller, 1969)

The Passing of the Aborigines   Daisy Bates (John Murray, 1966)

The Aborigines of Australia   J. W. Bleakley (Jacaranda Press, Brisbane, 1961)

The Australian Aborigines   A. P. Elkin (Angus and Robertson, 1964)

Yiwara: Foragers of the Australian Desert   Richard A. Gould (Collins, 1970)

Our Living Stone Age   Ion L. Idriess (Angus and Robertson, 1964)

Our Stone Age Mystery   Ion L. Idriess (Angus and Robertson, 1965)

The Australian Aborigines   Kenneth Maddock (Allen Lane, 1973)

Cooper's Creek   Alan Moorehead (Hamish Hamilton, 1953)

Adam in Ochre   Colin Simpson (Angus and Robertson, 1962)